Slaying Your Giants:

How to Have Massive Faith

By

Adam Houge

Slaying Your Giants: How to Have Massive Faith™
Copyright © 2014 by Adam Houge

Published by Living Tree Publishing in Harrisonburg, VA

All rights reserved worldwide. Permission is granted for quotations in all manner of religious assembly.

Portions of the text may be reprinted for use in small groups, church bulletins, orders of service, Sunday school lessons, church newsletters, and similar works, in the course of religious instruction, or services at a place of worship or other religious assembly with the following notice:

Slaying Your Giants: How to Have Massive Faith™
by Adam Houge
Scripture taken from the New King James Version®. Copyright © 1982 by Thomas Nelson, Inc. Used by permission. All rights reserved.

Also by Adam Houge

The 7 Most Powerful Prayers That Will Change Your Life Forever
The 7 Spiritual Habits That Will Change Your Life Forever
How to Memorize the Bible Quick and Easy in 5 Simple Steps
Choosing Words That Heal
I Know That God Is Good, But Why Am I Hurting So Much?
Miracles That Inspire

Table of Contents

The Giant Slayer

The thunder clapped overhead as the storm approached. The clouds were hanging ominously over the field as David drew near to the scene. A bear was dragging a sheep away from the fold in the distance, and the lamb in its jaws was screaming in pain and terror.

A streak of lightning flashed again, causing him to flinch from the brightness. Then he watched as the sheep managed to get away from the bear for a moment. But its departure was followed by an earth-shaking roar from the terrifying beast. David was mortified by the creature. But the Lord spoke into his heart, reassuring him that he needed to leave the flock to save the one that was lost.

David gritted his teeth and pressed forward. This animal wasn't about to get in between him and the will of God. Faith overtook him until fear no longer had a hiding place. Then he gripped the steely hilt of his blade as he prepared to strike. A downpour of rain burst across the field as he pushed forward in determination.

Then the animal took the sheep in its mouth again and headed for the woods as it ignored David's presence. His small stature could hardly pose a threat, it thought.

But as it fled from the rain David drew back his sword and hamstrung the bear with a mighty blow. A screeching bellow was heard from the creature before it turned on David. It locked its jaws on the boy's staff, narrowly missing his arm. But David grabbed it by the fur on its cheek and grimaced into its eyes as he thrust the blade through its throat.

The bear bellowed with a gurgle, then died at David's feet.

Suddenly, David was awakened from his memory by a gentle tap on the shoulder.

"Are you sure you want to do this?" said the voice. "He's been a warrior from his youth, and you're nothing but a youth!"

"Yes, your majesty," David replied. "I used to tend the flocks for my father, and when a lion or bear stole a sheep from the flock, I arose, struck it, and killed it. And if it turned to attack me, I'd grab it by the beard and thrust it through. The Lord, who saved me from the paws of animals, will save me from the hand of this man. I have killed both lion and bear, and this uncircumcised Philistine will be no different because he has defied the armies of the living God."

Saul was astonished. "Where could he have learned this faith?" he thought to himself. He remained speechless for a moment as he marveled at the young boy. But when he saw his confidence and the manner of Spirit who was upon him, he knew it was God's will and sent the boy forward.

Roaring laughter was heard from the giant. Goliath immediately took to mocking the boy who was approaching him. But when David wouldn't stop, Goliath knew that he intended to fight. He looked down at the youth in the distance.

"He's nothing but a boy!" he thought to himself. Then he hated David because he thought Israel was mocking him by sending a boy.

So Goliath howled at David, "Am I a dog, that you come to me with sticks?" Then he cursed David by his gods and said, "Come to me, and I will give your flesh to the birds of the air and the beasts of the field!"

This he said hoping to scare the boy off. He was in no mood to play along with Israel's game. But David gritted his teeth as he gripped the leathery sling in his hand.

"You come to me with a sword, with a spear, and with a javelin. But I come to you in the name of the LORD of hosts, the God of the armies of Israel, whom you have defied. This day the LORD will deliver you into my hand, and I will strike you and take your head from you. And this day I will give the carcasses of the camp of the Philistines to the birds of the air and the wild beasts of the earth, that all the earth may know that there is a God in Israel. Then all this assembly shall know that the LORD does not save with sword and spear; for the battle is the LORD's, and He will give you into our hands."

Goliath's mouth was hanging open at this point. He couldn't believe the boy's boldness. Then hate gripped his heart as he gnashed his teeth furiously. "I've had enough of your insolence, boy!" the towering warrior growled. Then charged at David in a rage.

But David reached into his pouch calmly, pulled out a smooth stone, and prepared his sling. The man approached quickly and prepared to swing, but David waited patiently for the perfect moment to strike. Then he prayed, "Lord, guide this stone to the weak spot in his armor!" And he slung the stone and struck the Philistine in his forehead. The stone hit him with such a force that it sank into his forehead, causing him to fall face-down on the ground.

Goliath lay there motionless while David approached. But the boy didn't take any chances; he drew Goliath's own sword and cut off the giant's head.

Victory Is Realized Through Small Steps

Consider sitting in David's shoes as the man approached to kill him. Can you imagine the fear that would have taken hold of you while you waited for the perfect moment to strike? As death approached you, one pounding step after another, how would you have felt, needing to wait?

But David didn't so much as flinch. Faith overtook him like a waterfall, and he killed the man as if he had been slaying giants his whole life.

God prepared him for this day and hour during his quiet moments with the Lord while he tended the flock. Likewise, God is preparing you for your own personal giants in life—circumstances that have yet to happen.

During these trials, God may tell you to wait. You'll watch disaster approach you one pounding step after another, but still God says, "Hold on… Be patient…" If you try to jump out of harm's way without God's approval, you will not be taking a leap of faith. Rather, you'll create an unforgettably worse trial.

Trust in God and wait for His saving power. He has appointed the giants in your life for you to overcome them and grow from them. Knowing, then, that God has determined to use His power to overcome your giants, why should you fear at all?

Beginning Faith with the End in Mind

In order to grow in faith, first we must understand the foundation of faith. Then, from the foundation up, we will build ourselves in Christ.

So what is faith?

"Now faith is the substance of things hoped for, the evidence of things not seen." Hebrews 11:1

Faith is evidence. Evidence suggests that it must be tangible. So we must have tangible works that prove our intangible faith.

But where does faith come from, and when should we have it?

"So then faith comes by hearing, and hearing by the word of God." Romans 10:17

This is where some Christians stumble. There are some who are taught to believe that if they believe anything hard enough, it will happen for them. If they believe with all their heart that God will pluck out the tree in their backyard and plant it in the sea, God will do it in fulfillment of the Scriptures.

But they are missing one key point: That faith must be in the words God says to you. Notice that Romans doesn't say, "Faith comes by reading." Rather, it says, "Faith comes by hearing." I'm not saying that we shouldn't have faith in the Scriptures. It is the word of God after all. But how Scripture is properly applied is spoken to us by the Holy Spirit on a moment by moment basis. When it is time to apply the Scripture, such as commanding a tree to be removed, the Holy Spirit will communicate that to us.

Ecclesiastes tells us that a time and a place exist for every activity under the sun. This holds true with faith. There is a time to have faith and a time not to have any. Do not trust in anything that God has not specifically said will happen. Jesus did say,

"...If you have faith as a mustard seed, you can say to this mulberry tree, 'Be pulled up by the roots and be planted in the sea,' and it would obey you." Luke 17:6

However, this Scripture wasn't spoken directly to you but to the disciples sitting nearby. So it isn't going to happen for you if the Holy Spirit hasn't confirmed that you should tell your tree or mountain to move. It isn't a question of the measure of your faith but of its accuracy. You can have all the faith in the world, but if it is not accurately placed in the words of the Spirit, nothing will happen.

Another example would be that of a man I knew of named Jeremy whose vehicle broke down while on his way to work. He prayed over his car, then told it in name of the Lord to start. After four attempts, it didn't start. Then he came to the conclusion that there was something wrong with his faith. He just needed to have more faith; then it would happen! So he prayed again and had all faith that God would do it. Then he closed his eyes, put the key in the ignition and said, "In the name of Jesus, I command you to work!" Without an ounce of doubt, he turned the key—but the car didn't start. In the end, he was late for work that day.

After everything was over, he decided, "It must not be God's will." But if he had started with the will of God and worked backward, he would not have had to waste his time yelling at his car and praying for things that weren't in God's will.

So the question is, "How is the will of God communicated to us?" Through the voice of the Holy Spirit. Hence, true faith comes by hearing the word of God. Whenever our faith lines up with the will of God, the Lord answers.

God's word can be split into two categories. There is the written word, upon which all Christianity is founded. Then there is the oral word, which is the voice of the Spirit, who explains to you in plain words how to apply the written word on a daily basis. By this we know that the oral word is as essential as the written word.

But it's interesting how some say, "It didn't happen because I must not have had enough faith." Jesus said that all it takes is a little mustard-seed-sized faith for miracles like these to happen—not mountain-sized faith. It doesn't take a mountain of faith to move a mountain. As the Scriptures tell us,

"So Jesus said to them, 'Because of your unbelief; for assuredly, I say to you, if you have faith as a <u>mustard seed</u>, you will say to this mountain, "Move from here to there," and it will move; and nothing will be impossible for you.'"

9

Matthew 17:20

In another scripture, Jesus calls a mustard seed the "smallest seed." So it only takes a little faith for great things to happen. Although God requires us to have great faith, He was making clear through this scripture that if you have even a little faith, nothing will be impossible for you. So the issue isn't always about the size of faith so much as what you're choosing to put your faith in.

"Well, I was putting my faith in Jesus that He would start my car," Jeremy said.

"Did Jesus say He would start your car?" his pastor asked.

"Well, no."

"So then, how did you know whether God was willing or not to start your car?"

"I didn't. … I just trusted Him. I thought if I had faith, it would happen."

"How can you have faith unless God tells you what He intends to do?"

Every time God speaks, our natural response must be with faith. If God hasn't spoken, then what are we trusting in? In ourselves and our personal hopes. But our faith must always be in His will. While we can pray for things and see large miracles happen, we cannot command the tree to uproot or the mountain to move unless God tells us to do so first.

Faith is meant to be about God. But it's funny how we make it about ourselves. "Well, if I only had a little more faith, then this or that would have happened!" Such a statement neglects the fact that God may not have been willing for the given thing to happen. It isn't about how much faith we have so much as it is about how faithful God is.

"I trust God won't let that happen to me" is a common sentiment I've heard. This is what a person may say when he or she is about to take a leap of faith, such as making a financial sacrifice, and is asked, "What will you do when it doesn't work out for you and you lose everything?"

"I trust God won't let that happen to me," he or she says. "He's faithful. He'll keep it from happening."

But how did God specifically tell you He wouldn't let it happen? How did God specifically tell you to make a sacrifice or take that leap of faith? If He didn't tell you, then you are hoping God will help, but you are not having faith. Faith comes by hearing, and God never told you to sacrifice or that He would help you if you did.

If you take a leap of faith without God telling you to do so, then you are jumping presumptuously in self-will. God will not bless that type of faith. If you want to take a leap of faith, then pray before doing anything and wait for the Lord's answer to determine if it is in His desire for you to make that leap in the first place. As it is written,

"Be anxious for nothing, but in everything by prayer and supplication, with thanksgiving, let your requests be made known to God…" Philippians 4:6

So the first step to having massive faith is that we must have accurate faith. Our faith must be in the will of

God, and in order for it to be in His will, we must become better listeners. The more you understand God's voice, the more effective your faith will be.

So take the time to grow in discernment, that His voice may be easier for you to hear. If you give God a thirty-minute daily devotion but then ignore Him for the rest of the day, how do you expect to hear Him with clarity when you need to hear His voice most? Hearing God is like exercising a muscle. The more you practice listening, the better you will hear and understand. But if you listen less often, it will be difficult to hear and understand the Lord when you need to most.

Knowing this, pay attention to the Spirit of the Lord throughout the day and not merely in a devotion. We are supposed to have devotions to recharge our batteries, but if we don't carry the charge with us, our ember will fade. Take the lesson of the devotion with you. Continue to pay attention to the presence of the Spirit when you step out of the secret place. Don't stop praying, but be faithful to pray continuously. As it is written,

"Continue earnestly in prayer, being vigilant in it with thanksgiving..." Colossians 4:2

Commit to a life of habitual prayer. Converse with God often, that you can be both attuned to His presence and sensitive to His voice. Put away the things that distract you from God so that you can be closer to Him.

Abstain from idleness. If it doesn't pertain to the Lord or edify you, then why are you partaking in that particular activity? That activity doesn't need to be blatant sin for it to be wrong. If it takes your focus off God, then it is a distraction. Every idol begins as a distraction. So if you're being distracted from God by something, then you have an idol.

You should be able both to meditate on the Spirit and to accomplish any activity you do, whether work or entertainment. This is especially so during entertainment, which is a time when your mind is resting and able to focus more easily. So if your entertainment is distracting you from God, then start looking for things that fill you with the Spirit and edify you.

By continuing to abide in the Spirit, you will hear God with greater clarity and apply your faith effectively. So take it to heart to worship and pray continually. Then, when you understand the will of God, you'll be able to overcome any obstacle. You'll enter trials with confidence, continue in them with joyful patience, and exit them with the same.

One of the most important steps to increasing your faith is to increase the time you spend growing in the Scriptures. If at all possible, set aside an hour every day to study. While this isn't always possible, the key is to take as much time as you can to spend growing in the word.

Some Christians have a habit of dedicating thirty minutes to reading; then, when the thirty minutes are over, they close their Bible and walk away. More often than not, the Scriptures were speaking out to them. If they are, then keep reading past thirty minutes and don't stop until they stop speaking to you. When the words pop out at you, this is the Holy Spirit speaking to you through the pages. When He does this, give Him as much time as He requires of you to sit and listen to Him.

How do you know how much time He requires? When you feel the words popping out at you from the scripture, He is speaking and requires you to listen. When they stop popping out at you, then stop reading. You will learn that you get more out of the Scriptures by memorizing and meditating on the pages that pop out at you than by focusing on the ones that don't.

Why is this? Because students get more from a course book as they follow along with the teacher. If they flip ahead and ignore his voice, then they learn nothing of significance. There is never a time for us to be self-taught in the Scriptures. Rather, we must all be God-taught. Even as Jesus said,

"It is written in the prophets, 'And they shall all be taught by God.' Therefore everyone who has heard and learned from the Father comes to Me." John 6:45

Knowing this, give more thoughtful attention to the scriptures that speak to you because the Lord Himself is actively teaching you through them in that moment.

A wise idea would be to write down everything you feel God is saying to you while you read. If the scriptures seem to come alive and other scriptures come to mind, know that God is teaching you and comparing each verse with others to provide you the whole teaching on the subject. As it is written,

"These things we also speak, not in words which

man's wisdom teaches but which the Holy Spirit teaches, comparing spiritual things with spiritual." 1 Corinthians 2:13

The Spirit will compare each spiritual lesson with each spiritual scripture. So take the time to write down everything He says. Do not write your own thoughts but discipline yourself only to write the things God says. Doing so will train you to understand the voice of God more clearly and help you to decipher between the words from your own heart and those from God's. The end result will be an ability to discern between your own will and God's, that you can submit to His will.

Taking it to heart to study your Bible will help your faith. Firstly, studying your Bible will help you understand the will of God; secondly, it will help you understand the nature of God; and thirdly, it will help you to understand His heart. When you understand His heart and nature, you'll understand when to apply faith properly and how to overcome every situation with confidence.

Whenever you need faith, always begin with the things that help you to understand what God is doing through the situation, what God requires of you, what He is telling you to do, and what His will is.

Total Surrender

Massive faith is on full display through total surrender to God's will. So take the plunge into a Spirit-directed life, laying your future completely in God's hands—the future of both your life that now is and that which is to come. Let Him decide what is best and what direction you should take. Let Him have full authority over you.

In order to live by perfect faith, first you must understand that God has plans for your life, plans that will give you a future and a hope if you follow them. But if you don't follow them, then you are not living for Christ. Christian literally means "follower of Christ." So in order to be Christian, first we must allow Jesus to take the lead through His Spirit. That God has plans for you is evident. For it is written,

"For I know the thoughts that I think toward you, says the LORD, thoughts of peace and not of evil, to give you a future and a hope." Jeremiah 29:11

The original Hebrew word for 'thoughts' in this verse is 'machăshâbâh.' This word literally means "thoughts, intentions, purpose, or plan." Hence, some versions of the Bible translate this verse as saying, "I know the plans I have for you."

God has plans for you. He has a future in mind—a future of peace both in this life and in the next. All you have to do is believe. He also has specific works He wants you to do, including both occasional, great works and daily, small works. If you're not circumspect in your walk, paying attention to the soft voice of the Spirit, then you'll never know what those works are or when they need to be accomplished. In order to walk in righteousness, we must walk in faith. In order to walk in faith, we must walk in the Spirit while obeying His voice. Therefore, it is required of us to work in the Spirit, that the Lord may operate through us. And as it is written,

"For we are His workmanship, created in Christ Jesus for good works, which God prepared beforehand that we should walk in them." Ephesians 2:10

In order to live out the works God has for us, we must be led by His Spirit. In order to be led by the Spirit, first we must hear His voice and obey. So sensitize yourself to the Spirit, and surrender. Let go of your own heart and let Him dictate your life, not only in the major plans of life but even in the little day-to-day tasks as well. You'll find that He will have you love, serve, pray, and worship daily while beckoning you to rest in Him frequently throughout the day.

It's easy to become distracted by the scores of things around us. There are many needful tasks that call for our attention. But rather than accomplishing the task and determining to seek the Lord afterward, seek Him while you accomplish the task. Pray and abide during every activity. If during anything you do, you cannot abide at the same time, then God doesn't want you devoting your attention to that activity today.

But if there is any activity that you can accomplish while praying at the same time, then He wants you doing that activity. Surrender your desires to do something else, and continue to do the things God is calling you to do, whether work, serving, taking care of children, or resting and praying.

You'll find over time that it will be difficult to abide while you do a certain activity. This is God telling you to take a break, pull away from the distractions around you, and be recharged in the Spirit.

So, for example, if a mother were to wash the dishes for her children, at first she may be able to abide and focus on the Spirit through prayer and worship. But then, after finishing them, she proceeds to wash the counter and sweep the floor, only to notice that it has become difficult to focus on God. At this point, she has to ask herself which is more important: her relationship with God or scrubbing the floor.

Don't be tempted to finish the task at hand. Take a fifteen-minute break to be alone with God; then pick up where you left off.

This, particularly, is an issue for stay-at-home mothers. Those who work can find the rest they need during scheduled breaks. During those times, rather than talking idly, it would be better to pray or worship silently, spending time in the presence of God to be recharged. But stay-at-home mothers never seem to take breaks.

If this describes you, take the time to consider: Would you take breaks at work? Then why not at home?

You need it! Your job is extremely important and can be very taxing on the body, spirit, and emotions—especially if you have multiple young children or toddlers.

The problem a mother has is that God has given her a servant's heart. She tends never to think of herself or her own needs, which isn't wrong. However, she needs to realize that spending time to recharge her spirit, while not a need like eating or sleeping, is nonetheless God's command for her—if she is to love the Lord above all else.

Since the day her babies were born, she has been having sleepless nights, tending to her children's every beck and call. But now she needs to remember that God comes first.

Remember that we are commanded to love the Lord our God with all our heart, soul, mind, and strength, but our neighbor as ourselves. So love your children as yourself and put God first. Take breaks and rest in the Spirit. Fifteen minutes' rest never hurt anybody!

No matter who you are or what you're doing—whether at work or entertaining yourself—you need to take breaks to continue in the Spirit. Examine yourself in this: Are you pushing yourself too hard? Do you strive to accomplish what you think needs to be done or what God is telling you to do? Do you allow God to direct and lead your day so that you accomplish what He wants you to do in His timeframe?

Living for His will in every little activity will change your life! That we should be led by God is evident. For it is written,

"For as many as are led by the Spirit of God, these are sons of God." Romans 8:14

And also,

"But if you are led by the Spirit, you are not under the law." Galatians 5:18

If you are led by the Spirit, then God is operating through you. When Jesus works through you, you become like Jesus, who is above the law. Therefore, they who are led by the Spirit are justified. But if you are never led by the Spirit and instead live according to your will, then you are not justified. Even as it is written,

"And you have done worse than your fathers, for behold, each one follows the dictates of his own evil heart, so that no one listens to Me." Jeremiah 16:12

And also,

"...so that there may not be among you man or woman or family or tribe, whose heart turns away today from the LORD our God, to go and serve the gods of these nations, and that there may not be among you a root bearing bitterness or wormwood; and so it may not happen, when he hears the words of this curse, that he blesses himself in his heart, saying, 'I shall have peace, even though I follow the dictates of my heart'—as though the drunkard could be included with the sober." Deuteronomy 29:18–19

The gods of this nation are self-actualization and wealth. In trying to further yourself, pave your own future, and plan your own destiny, you have become your own god. These are His responsibilities, however, and if you don't trust Him with them, then you are not walking by faith. If we are only justified by faith yet refuse to walk in it, are we therefore saved? How can we claim to be saved and be our own god at the same time? A walk with Jesus isn't about applying what we think is the Bible is telling us to apply. Rather, it is about obeying the Holy Spirit, who teaches us daily how to walk in Christ and apply the Bible. If we do not listen to His voice, then we are not walking in faith.

We operate in the Spirit when we listen to His voice, believe, and obey. Thus, these are the works of faith that justify us. As we read,

"But do you want to know, O foolish man, that faith without works is dead? Was not Abraham our father justified by works when he offered Isaac his son on the altar? Do you see that faith was working together with his works, and by works faith was made perfect? And the Scripture was fulfilled which says, "Abraham believed God, and it was accounted to him for righteousness." And he was called the friend of God. You see then that a man is justified by works, and not by faith only. Likewise, was not Rahab the harlot also justified by works when she received the messengers and sent them out another way? For as the body without the spirit is dead, so faith without works is dead also." James 2:20–26

Perfect faith requires action. If you truly believe something, then you need to act on it. You need to do something with your faith if you want it to be real and tangible.

Therefore, Beloved, surrender to the Spirit and obey

His voice. For in so doing, you will be walking in the faith that justifies and saves. Remember, we said faith is the evidence of unseen things. In order for it to be evident, we must have tangible works to prove our intangible faith. These are not the works of the law, which do not justify. The works of the law are on display in Christians who read their Bible and try to apply it the way they think is best. They study hard; then, when they know what a passage means, they press hard to apply it in their life rather than allowing the Holy Spirit to teach them when and how to do it on a daily basis.

But the works of faith are on full display in those who are led by the Spirit, being vigilant to His voice and swift to obey. Faith, not our own opinions on how the Bible should be applied, justifies us. So those who apply the Scriptures the way they feel is best are not pursuing a deeper relationship with the Lord, nor are they exhibiting the faith that saves. But those who abide in the Spirit daily, and apply the Scriptures in the way He plainly tells them to do, grow more intimate with Him. They walk in the faith that is perfect.

So surrender everything you are to God. Lay your entire future in His hands. Learn to be led by His Spirit— it will change your life. The more you listen to God, the more opportunity you'll have to exercise faith. The more you exercise faith, the more you'll grow in it. Therefore, the more you are led by the Spirit, the more faith you will have, and the more you'll experience both the love and the power of God in your life.

Total Release

Stop worrying! There is a statistic that one out of every four Americans dies from a stress-related illness before the age of sixty.

Consider the size of your church. Take the number of members under sixty years old and divide by four. You can't include any who are over sixty years because they've already made it past the statistical age. Your answer represents how many people will die before sixty because of stress.

Jesus says that you can't turn a single hair on your head white or black, and He says you can't add a cubit to your stature. The Scriptures also say, "…Do not fret—it only causes harm" (Psalm 37:8). Fretting really does cause a lot of harm. It causes harm mentally because you're dwelling on negativity. It causes harm physically because it puts stress on the body, and stress kills. It also causes harm spiritually because, rather than being built up and edified by faith, you're dwelling on fear.

Never fear a situation but always persist in faith. God is your salvation in everything; believe that He will deliver you. Remember also that the Scriptures say,

"There is no fear in love; but perfect love casts out fear, because fear involves torment. But he who fears has not been made perfect in love. We love Him because He first loved us." 1 John 4:18–19

God gives you everything out of love. If you're fearing, then you're not being made perfect in love. Remember that we love Him because He first loved us. So press onward in your faith and do not give power to doubt!

There's a difference between knowing and believing something. Just because you know God loves you doesn't mean it always feels as if He does. But if you believe and persist in faith, you'll find a change taking place in your heart.

When difficult circumstances lead you to feel as if God doesn't love you, you need to believe that He does and that He is still good. For God gives us trials to grow us in Christ and increase our faith. Salvation, in turn, comes by faith. As we read,

"For by grace you have been saved through faith, and that not of yourselves; it is the gift of God." Ephesians 2:8

Therefore, Beloved, know that when trials and tribulation come your way, God is securing your salvation through love. Not everything God gives us will be pleasurable. Our flesh is contrary to God, and God is contrary to our flesh, after all. He will give us what we need to edify us in the Spirit. Even if that requires some suffering in the flesh, He will give us what is best for our current spiritual need. He will teach you through your trial, that you may walk with wisdom and in the path of eternal life.

Our fathers have disciplined us to walk uprightly. They teach us how to be responsible so we can have food on our table, good relationships, and less suffering in life. Yet it all begins with something that isn't desirable: discipline.

Discipline is never fun but, rather, always painful one way or another, whether emotionally or physically. Yet these things are given to us that we may have growth and find life. If we were not trained how to live responsibly, we'd end up constantly suffering brokenness until we figured life out through the school of hard knocks.

God also disciplines us. His chastisement can be painful for a time, but the benefit is eternal. Because He cares for us and loves us, He gives us what we need for growth whether we like it or not. So no matter what, believe that God loves you.

During the hardest moments in life, Satan loves to tempt a believer to think that God doesn't love him or her. But the way to resist the devil is through steadfast faith. Do not give way to the enemy or let doubt linger in your mind. Rather, dwell on the love of God and believe that, no matter what, He gives you all things out of love.

Consider also that it is written,

"So He humbled you, allowed you to hunger, and fed you with manna which you did not know nor did your fathers know, that He might make you know that man shall not live by bread alone; but man lives by every word that proceeds from the mouth of the LORD." Deuteronomy 8:3

God allows you to go through circumstances of suffering so you can learn to live by His word. Notice that it doesn't just say "written word." Instead, it says that you may live by every word that proceeds out of the mouth of the Lord. This includes both the written words and the words that His Spirit speaks to you daily.

Remember also that we are justified by faith, and faith comes from every word that He speaks. Therefore, God is telling you through this scripture that He allows you to suffer so you can learn to be led by the Spirit and justified in everything you do.

This we have also seen in Jesus' life. For it is written,

"...who, in the days of His flesh, when He had offered up prayers and supplications, with vehement cries and tears to Him who was able to save Him from death, and was heard because of His godly fear, though He was a Son, yet He learned obedience by the things which He suffered." Hebrews 5:7–8

Likewise, we learn obedience to His voice through the things we suffer. There are many who tell you that God will never give you more than you can bear. Then they recite the scripture that says,

"No temptation has overtaken you except such as is common to man; but God is faithful, who will not allow you to be tempted beyond what you are able, but with the temptation will also make the way of escape, that you may be able to bear it." 1 Corinthians 10:13

But notice that this verse says He never allow you to be *tempted* beyond what you're able to bear. This scripture suggests that God will never allow you to be tempted into sin without providing a way out. That way, you're free will can be perfect rather than being forced into one decision or another.

But in regard to trials and the giants of life, nowhere does it say God will not give you more than you can bear. On the contrary, you'll find that God gives you far more than you could ever imagine bearing in your trials. That way, you'll learn to surrender your circumstances to Him, so He can bear them up on His shoulders.

God will always give you more than you can bear on your own. Why? Because He is your way of escape. Then, by relying on Him, you realize that you can bear the burden because Jesus is doing it through you. So God will allow you to suffer, but only so you can learn to rest in and be strengthened by Him.

In every trial, God intends to do good to you. Even as we read,

"And we know that all things work together for good to those who love God, to those who are the called according to His purpose." Romans 8:28

Job suffered a devastating loss. Financially, he was bankrupt. His children died, and his wife despised him for it, blaming him as the cause. His friends reviled him to the point of tears. He was left broken and alone in an ash heap, waiting and begging for the faithfulness of God. In the end, the Lord revealed Himself to Job. As it is written,

"Then the LORD answered Job out of the <u>whirl-wind</u>, and said..." Job 38:1

The Hebrew word for 'whirlwind' literally means 'storm' or 'tornado.' So much as in Job's case, God is there in the midst of the storms of your life to teach you and comfort you through it all. He is in the middle of the disaster, at the very heart of it, to comfort you. But He will not end the storm until He has stripped away everything that is necessary for you to grow in Him as you ought. While this may be painful, remember the scripture that says,

"Every branch in Me that does not bear fruit He takes away; and every branch that bears fruit He prunes, that it may bear more fruit." John 15:2

Sometimes it seems as if every time we step out in faith, something goes wrong. After taking to heart the responsibility of honoring God, we get slapped with a trial. Why? Because God sees our fruit and wants us to bear more. So He will teach us through suffering to be obedient, even as He did with Jesus.

But God does these things for the sake of your eternal life. With careful consideration and much forethought, He permits the trials of life in order to prune us, to grow us, and ultimately to bless us. By this we can see He cherishes us.

When we understand that God intends good for us through our trials, they become easier to bear. Therefore, Beloved, endure with patience, knowing that God doesn't permit your trials to save you from them but to bless you far beyond them. As it is written,

"For our light affliction, which is but for a moment, is working for us a far more exceeding and eternal weight of glory..." 2 Corinthians 4:17

And also,

"Indeed we count them blessed who endure. You have heard of the perseverance of Job and seen the end intended by the Lord—that the Lord is very compassionate and merciful." James 5:11

Since you know that God intends good through your heartbreak, surrender to Him happily. Learn to rejoice in your trials through faith. Worship Him even as Job did. As we read,

"Then Job arose, tore his robe, and shaved his head; and he fell to the ground and worshiped. And he said: 'Naked I came from my mother's womb, and naked shall I return there. The LORD gave, and the LORD has taken away; blessed be the name of the LORD.' In all this Job did not sin nor charge God with wrong." Job 1:20–22

God calls us to rejoice always and in everything. Rejoicing in trials is a tremendous act of faith because, in so doing, you are proclaiming both that you believe God is good in everything He does and that He will save you from the situation. But that we should rejoice in every situation is evident. For it is written,

"Rejoice in the Lord always. Again I will say, rejoice!" Philippians 4:4

And also,

"My brethren, count it all joy when you fall into various trials, knowing that the testing of your faith produces patience. But let patience have its perfect work, that you may be perfect and complete, lacking nothing." James 1:2–4

Endure all things with joy, knowing that God intends not only to save you from suffering but also to bless you in your trials. God would never give you a trial or an unsurmountable mountain in life unless He intended to be your strength to overcome—and to give you something better in the end. That blessing may not be physical, however; it may be eternal wisdom gained from your circumstances. But God would never give you any trial if there weren't something better to be had through it. The blessing in the end will always be greater than the means to get there.

So release your life to God instead of worrying about tomorrow. Let Him plan it for you; then everything will work together for good because you love Him.

Facing Your Giants

Everyone has experienced a moment when faith seems impossible—one of those David and Goliath moments. It's easy to be intimidated by the size of your foe. But if God has called you to the battle, then assuredly He will fight for you, that He may be glorified.

God doesn't just permit these difficult situations in life but appoints them for your sake so you can learn from them and grow thereby. He appoints them to test you and refine your faith, that through your circumstances you will learn to rest in Christ at all times. When you do this, He can work through you continually. He doesn't give you these difficult situations for you to learn that He'll only be your strength when everything falls apart. Rather, He would have you learn that He has always been your strength, so you would learn to rely on Him more.

It is a continual Sabbath to which He calls you—a rest from the works of the flesh and from operating in your own strength, that God can work for you and be glorified. He, like any loving father, is compelled to provide for you. So let Him provide hope and salvation as He does the work while you rest softly and gently in His presence.

In David's situation, God raised up Goliath to be in the position he was in, and to have the stature he had, that God would be glorified through his destruction by the hand of David. This situation was foreordained so that

David could rise to power. This concept can also be seen in an earlier scripture. As it is written,

"For the Scripture says to the Pharaoh, 'For this very purpose I have raised you up, that I may show My power in you, and that My name may be declared in all the earth.' Therefore He has mercy on whom He wills, and whom He wills He hardens." Romans 9:17–18

The Lord raised up Pharaoh to oppose Moses and Israel. That way He could be glorified when He saved His children by His might. Likewise, God has appointed the giants of your life with the intention of overcoming them for you and teaching you to rely on Him through them. He allows these circumstances so that He can be glorified through them. As we read,

"Now as Jesus passed by, He saw a man who was blind from birth. And His disciples asked Him, saying, 'Rabbi, who sinned, this man or his parents, that he was born blind?' Jesus answered, 'Neither this man nor his parents sinned, but that the works of God should be revealed in him.'" John 9:1–3

Afterward, Jesus healed the man of his blindness, and He was glorified as a result. Similarly, God will permit certain circumstances in your life that will glorify Him. Others will look at you and know that there is no way you could overcome them by yourself. Then, when you do overcome them, they know that it was God who worked through you. This is a good witness for the unbeliever, enabling them to see the power of Jesus alive and at work in you. Because when the living power of God delivers you from your circumstances, it gives testimony to the truth that Jesus is alive, risen, and Lord over all.

As it is written,

"But we have this treasure in earthen vessels, that the excellence of the power may be of God and not of us. We are hard-pressed on every side, yet not crushed; we are perplexed, but not in despair; persecuted, but not forsaken; struck down, but not destroyed—always carrying about in the body the dying of the Lord Jesus, that the life of Jesus also may be manifested in our body. For we who live are always delivered to death for Jesus' sake, that the life of Jesus also may be manifested in our mortal flesh. So then death is working in us, but life in you." 2 Corinthians 4:7–12

When the life of Christ is operating in us to overcome obstacles the world cannot, they are compelled to stand in awe. It makes them pause for a moment as they absorb the fact that Jesus just saved you—and that He can save them, too. So your giants were appointed, like Jesus' cross. Bear your cross so that you can be the example of Christ and bring life to others, who will believe in Christ through watching you overcome your trials.

When you look up at the mountains of your life, they may seem insurmountable. And that's because they are! You can't possibly climb them or overcome them—not under your own strength, at least.

But the Lord appointed them so that the only way out of your circumstances is through Him. That way, you may learn to rely on Him so that He may be glorified and others may see the testimony of Jesus as they watch Him save you mightily.

Goliath was raised up for David's faith to wipe him out. Even so, God is preparing your faith now and anticipating that it will wipe out your giants in life. So take it to heart to grow constantly in faith. Draw near to the Lord and pray and abide without ceasing.

If you pray that God would increase your faith, He will. But be aware that He will increase it by giving you opportunities for faith. Some will be good situations, and others will be bad. Expect trials when you pray for more faith. But as you learn from each trial, they will become less necessary and will taper off.

So take each teaching to heart, that you don't have to relearn old lessons. Many trials can be avoided by continually practicing the things that the Lord teaches you. Some trials may even end sooner if you learn the lesson more quickly.

Ultimately, if you know your giants have been appointed by God for you to overcome them, why would you fear them? Be bold in your faith and take heart. For the Lord intends to save you from your giants and bless you with something greater.

I'd Love to Hear from You!

As an author, I regard the feedback of my readers highly. When considering a book, many people weigh reviews in the balance.

If you enjoyed this book, please consider helping others to make an informed decision. Leaving a review can help spread the message of the gospel, increase others' faith through these books, and be a great way to support this ministry for free!

19592723R00029

Made in the USA
Middletown, DE
27 April 2015